MEZZANINE

poems by

Susan Kay Anderson

Finishing Line Press
Georgetown, Kentucky

MEZZANINE

ACKNOWLEDGMENTS

"It Is Bear-like," "Bears and Berries," "It often feels like wasted time," and "The summer bell rings," first appeared on Tom Clark's blog: *Tom Clark Beyond The Pale*.

"My Father Wanted The West," *Rain Bird 25th Anniversary Issue; Caliban Online*

"Mid-life dream(s) (continued)," *Caliban Online*

"Dreams (continued)," *Caliban Online*

"No Boxing Day," *Caliban Online, Tom Clark Beyond The Pale*

"It Begins Then To Be Possible To Imagine," *Caliban Online, Tom Clark Beyond The Pale*

"Conference of the Clouds," *Caliban Online*

"Man's West Once," *Barrow Street Press 4 X 2 Project*

"Mezzanine" (page 10), *Timothy McSweeney's Internet Tendency*
Small sections of "Mezzanine" were part of the manuscript, "The Body Of No Moment," winner of a Jovanovich Award, University of Colorado-Boulder.

Page 29, *Mojave River Review*
Page 30, *Carolina Quarterly*
Page 41 and 51, *Caliban Online*

Publisher: Leah Maines
Editor: Christen Kincaid
Cover Art: Susan Kay Anderson
Author Photo: Susan Kay Anderson
Cover Design: Leah Huete

Printed in the USA on acid-free paper.
Order online: www.finishinglinepress.com
also available on amazon.com

Author inquiries and mail orders:
Finishing Line Press
P. O. Box 1626
Georgetown, Kentucky 40324
U. S. A.

Table of Contents

Where is my West?
How do I find it?

Fire Cipher

> *Someday, somewhere—anywhere, unfailingly, you'll find yourself, and*
> *that, and only that, can be the happiest or the bitterest hour of your life.*

—Pablo Neruda

that and only that
called out
from a tree
near Walla Walla
that trip
from Missoula
from an everyday pine
or was it Raven's
green wings
dry fever

where it is winter
where it is a river

I spent an hour
depending upon
that view

Night is another time. A place of night hawks.

I work graveyard shift cleaning a building on the university campus. It is the Architecture and Allied Arts building. In my job as a custodian, sometimes, rounding a corner, I feel as if I've rounded that corner a million times and also never. There is also the matter of the mezzanine. It hangs beneath a floor, or it can be up a short flight of stairs. A mezzanine may have a balcony. If you are a person standing outside a room

and you want to go to the mezzanine
first you need to find it
and once you are there
you may not realize
that you have found
a place to look up, out, and back.

The grey cement floors become a shiny cave, my dust mop is a bear's fur that leaves the place polished with a sheen of *Baerenschliffe*, bear shimmer that beautifies and brings in more light. My mind is a butterfly. Dreams are being made of nothing but paper, glue, and paperboard materials all around.

My father wanted the West.
When he was little he got cowboys
and Indians and also a boy
with a moon for a head,
pineapple spikes for hair.
He wanted joy and sustained surprise.
That's what he got
with Moon Boy just by taking a look.

This made sense. My father,
showing his teeth, genuine agates.
His hair, wild, scraggly oaks
and smooth corn husks. A scent
rising off his clothes like buckskin
and eagle feathers in the fancy dance
he did across the country.

It wasn't as if he were lazy
but he wanted the West to come
to him, only, instead, it passed
through him and out the other side—
through his body towards Mom, me,
and my sisters swirling like satellites
around a heavenly body.

Mezzanine

I am familiar

                    with the way I think.
                    My thoughts
                    have a definite order
                    that is my own,
                    and any deviation
                    is noticeable.

They say that if you clean at night you're cleaning up after the dead. If you clean up, then it is for them that you're doing it, wiping away the evidence of life.

The light could go in and out.   Shadows of the shadow self
move light from below
support its shape

                                        the shape of a butterfly.

I saw how it looked.   It looked like danger
if you somehow got caught   inside its intricate weaving.

I speak the password primeval

to the abbreviated   (trash)

cleaning up   the daytime actions
short now
in the endless night

plants, stones, utensils
          each with its own feeling   during existence.

after the dead

Greg, another night custodian, is dying. I came back from vacation and found out he had been sick and was in the hospital. He is 67 and has cancer of the liver, lungs, and colon. He is a vet, did not serve overseas, and instead, was stationed in Pendleton, Oregon.

exchanging	full bags
all	
the empty	fast food containers
slipping	new ones into
empty	time

The news wasn't that great about Greg and he didn't want me telling the other custodians a thing about his cancer, about his procedure, and about how he wouldn't be back. Walking around without him on 1st Floor was an empty feeling, even with all the users in the building walking through and up the elevator to 3rd and 4th to finish architecture projects, design projects. The memory of him sitting in his rather palatial custodian closet.

This was at the hospital. Greg let out some gas and told me he was glad I had visited but he was getting real tired, said to hang in there and remember what he said about the toilets, *only the rim and only one swipe, then leave it.*

Walking with Lili and Lena before shift they asked and I told them, although it was just the one time. The one time they asked and the one time I told, even though I could feel Greg listening in behind the big red cedar and a little along the bushes bordering Pacific. There

was snow on the ground and I was glad Greg would miss all the slush and icing-over of footprints and tracked-in debris onto the entrance mats. He wouldn't need to vacuum them.

All in all, all told, Dan left up Greg's collage decorating the walls of his closet. Magazine pages and posters of football players,

Steve Prefontaine, churches and cathedrals in Europe, close-ups of alpine wild flowers.

> I thought I had placed it just so
> between third and fourth
> yesterday when I was
> community minded and jotting down
> my plans for a cube—
>
> one centimeter ago
> everything was red.
>
> The project could not fail
> everything riding on it
> especially the in between
> where I spoke to the planet
> asked for it to return
> to its normal self
> and not all this funny business.

exchanging
all
the empty
slipping
empty

full bags

fast food containers

time

> If you clean up, then it is for them that you're doing it
> on the third floor mezzanine.

Just within the front entrance is an artwork called "Elements of Time."
It looks like the Periodic Table Of Elements, but instead of elements
such as minerals and gasses and such, it is comprised of how we spend
our time: sleeping, working, making love (it doesn't say this, I made
this up), and is written with catch phrases such as "time off," and "time
out" (it doesn't say this either, again, I've made this up—the elements
state emotions—loss, joy, worry). It is a little like a slap in science's
face, a little like a cutesy way of abbreviating our actions, feelings,
and concepts; making this "periodic table" fleeting and superficial.
I wonder about its color, an industrial green color, but also blended
hues of the university's sports colors (mixing Kelly green and yellow to
make a mossy color) the exact same color as the bottles

of disinfectant we use in cleaning

a butterfly skeleton.

Made of the forest, its trees.
Covered because of dust.

All rolled into a flat pack.
The colors were mixed.

They interact with daylight.
At night you can see.

The more you look at color
the more you understand

the movement of color
through time and space.

This is applied to the building environment.
It is a book that's not a book.

There are duplicate plates
flaps that flip. Flap.

The fresh air is a rush

after breathing disinfectants.

64 for the floors
65 to spot clean

and the seldom-used 66.

The face of plastic   does not change

my feelings.

Was it two minutes ago   or was it ten years?

I am grabbing   the rotting contents
that speak the language   of the Mezzanine:

plastic wrappers, plastic utensils, paper board, foam board, tissue
paper, wood, paper coffee cups and their plastic lids, pencils, notes,
notebooks, thin wooden sticks, plastic bags.

Was it half a century ago
or was it last year?

Our foster sister
posted a photo   of the moon in Fairbanks
yesterday
said that she could see   the moon's face.

I remember her visiting us   camping at Tahoe

I remember the dogfights in Nome

but also the boardwalk, the army jacket, the nuggets, the bear in a cage, the ice, the break-up, the huskies, the school, the jackets, the mukluks, the kuspuks, the pilot bread, the drunk babysitter and the passed-out boyfriend, the blueberries (huckleberries really), the cabin called Teetering-on-the-Brink, Chicken Hill, the Chungs, the 8-track player, the time grandma peed her pants from laughing, the theater, Elvis's '68 Comeback Special, Commando Cody: Sky Marshal of the Universe, the Tundra, the Lutheran Church, the Methodist Church, the TV channel, the albums, the visitors (Kathleen Kennedy), the camping, the driftwood, the rivers, the fishing trips, the citizens of Nome, the wanderers.

People wandered about in Nome. Maybe because I was nine and reading Nancy Drews, I was most interested in the mysteries of these people—the clues never led anywhere but death. Clouds of mosquitoes wanted our bodies all summer long. One babysitter told me to breathe only through my nose during winter. Another wanted my parents to bail her out of jail because her class at school was going to take a field trip there. At the library, there was a gold nugget displayed next to the Nancy Drews. The Nome Nugget, as big as a dog's head. A restaurant had the same name.

A siren blew every day at noon. All the dogs howled to it. There was salmon to eat. There were cases of canned food. One time, our dog, Shumagin, got into a vicious fight at a camp out party with my parents. I saw his eye pulled out by another dog. I saw the optic nerve.

I would also tell Denise and Robert about Mango Man in Kailua, Hawaii. He is ghost-like because his body is halfway in this dimension and halfway out, with his mind tagging along. Most of Nome's citizens were like Mango Man. They wandered about the town in winter and summer, minimally present, but always seemed to be on their way to somewhere else.

she was sleeping
in the tent
passed out
from the heat and the night
at Harrah's with Mom
going to see Tom Jones in concert.

We watched while
a man dived into the clear cold water.
We sat on the piney beach with Mom
in the golden sand. Mom was topless.
We were so embarrassed. Please
put on your top, we said. That man will see.
She lifted her arms above her head and stretched.
European style, she said.
It took about a minute to get too cold
jumping in and out of the water, ignoring her.
Our fingers were so blue the sun did not warm them.

El Dorado, the man of gold
jumped into the icy lake. Pine pitch
glittering with gold dust
stuck to his body. It kept him warm.
After he jumped out of the water
the gold sank to the bottom of the lake.
The subjects on the shore clapped wildly.
He must have looked like a golden human fish.

On the beach near Nome we took Kathleen Kennedy
and her friend Sophie for a picnic the second day
they stayed with us. My dad smoked a cigarette
then another, watching the topless teenagers
jumping in and out of the waves. Their breasts
larger than the hands that held them. Dad's
cigarette stub glowing dangerously close to his fingers.
Kathleen trying to pop corn after the salmon roast,
using only salt, no oil, her method. The popcorn

burning black as the abandoned starts of driftwood.
A dogfight started with our dog. Distraction.

Josef Albers' plates
are on view during the week
from eight to five
in the first floor gallery.

At night they disappear.

In their absence
empty frames wait
hanging in space.

To become

butterflies and their skeletons

reindeer and their antlers

apple halves

dwelling places

islands.

[Entryway]

In the safety of the diorama there is never
any trouble. Across from the Hope Diamond
(reproduction) I'll get married. To myself.
Lie naked on the crushed velvet and slowly
paint tattoos of leaves all over my shoulders.
My newly married hair. My eyes will never leave
the Hope Diamond in its case. I crouch by the stream
in the High Plains Diorama and take a bath
lick the lint off my back. Turn this way
and that. In the safety of the diorama
there is no wind. After hours I will close my eyes
like a bat's. Sleep like a baby. The air is the same air
night and day. For food, my friends will help.
The Jaguar With His Prey. The European Hedgehog.
The Fish Eagle.

Out in the middle of nowhere near Nome,
out in an acre of wind, there was an old cabin
with a greenhouse out back. Dirt in the small boxes
but no glass on the roof. Just the frame.
The wind was like a person with frozen mossy fingers
who brushed and crushed the dirt. Sent it over
the rolling tundra. The dirt ended up
in the Nome Public Library in the form of a huge gold nugget.
It had its own case. Right next to the Nancy Drews.
I consider it to be the first diorama I saw
and also the last. Because I took the gold
and never looked back. I have been safe ever since.

[Marooned. Marooning. Marooned in a dream.]

The island was alive
although nobody wanted it to be.
Not really. They sang and danced
about its beginning and the start of things

that otherwise came to be
and the island didn't give a shit either
it was purported to be
all-seeing all-knowing. Was I
supposed to take Tina's advice
and not go there? I ignored her before
but in miniscule increments
that I thought had never counted. Until
I began growing a stone inside me. Plus.
These past eight almost nine years
when she turned the tables
stunning in her ignoring finery.
Albert said cool things although they were
projected from an imaginary radio station
dialed to somewhere beyond the 34th parallel.
Tina. Microdot. Dot. Someday we'll call
and be real sisters. You won't be jealous of my nothing.
Mom, Dad, shrinking. I can fit into his new shirts.
Mom's not at all. Tina, fall from a tree.
Be a monkey nut again. Nutty for salad. Dave Matthews
can keep his rushing logic. Dr. Phil his whiny magic.

[Corner]
You, you there
close your mouth
and only breathe
through your nose
else your lungs
will freeze
walking home from school.
Alapaa, it's cold.

The Vietnam War was on T.V.
on Nome's one cable channel,
We had to rush home to watch.

[Stairwell]

Two months ago

Elvina was so sick

almost died of botulism

because of the *muktuk*

    stowed under the house

    for the fermentation process.

Her sister, Mathilde
also got sick
fifteen years ago
from salmon eggs.

Not cold enough now
not cold enough to live
to have the food
satisfy the cravings—

[Window]

Yes, she stayed with us
on the weekends
away from Beltz High
so your father and I could
go to parties at Brian's.
That's when I would disappear
into the magic of Chicken Hill
a few blocks away.

The students and the other users
fill the stairwells with sand.
The dust. Stardust. The skin they shed.
Their hair.

[Elevator]

I gave myself to the moment,
I heard what I wanted to hear.

It was a moment of footsteps and quiet air.

It was another world. A world that stopped moving, everything still

the evening a grey green

mauve

and hushed, except for that buzzing. All the bees swarming
around my ear. My ear was so friendly to them. I tried to catch up.

I have not shed them at all.

They've dug into the old hillside

and

are waiting

patiently

for me to return.

Silence is not really silent
on the busy tundra.

Owls' wings and small creatures.
The other angels against the moon.
I could not open my eyes to it and to that.   I knew
About silence   but thought about those bees,
right against my ear again, right beside my cheek.

Would I give myself over to their spell?   The spell of the bees.
Would I even hear them
so close up? How could we discuss this
in a logical way?
The bees need food.   They like honey.
Give them some.

I'll be listening for it.

In the aftermath of nothing, I've found a little something,

crumbs,
signs.

I'll take your hand

like someone alive and living

in the place love exists

password:
raw honey.

Honey inside the buzzing.
Dripping inside the comb.
Sealing, coverings, membranes

so easily sucked away, licked off

ear, mouth, teeth to tongue,
to lips and skin. I found
your raw honey explorations

true

what they say

about nature's food

complete

without interference. Go now
and tell me later
what else you've found.

[Alcove]

It seemed impossible that earth were anything but gardens, pools, architectures, and splendorous forms. Every hundred paces a tower cleft the air; to the eye their color was identical, yet the first of all was yellow, and the last, scarlet, so delicate were the gradations and so long the series.

— Jorge Luis Borges

Yellow

I was that yellow flower
you held
a petal among all the other petals.
I would unfold and unfold again.
Can't you see my scented idea?

What if you
planted me here

with the sage and cat tails
at the edge of the marsh
where I could grow into a tree.

I'd bear fantastic fruit. The fruit would fall every year at the
edge of the lake where animals eat and eat.

Tell me what you have named me.

It is yellow flower. It is nickels rubbed together.

Tell me what you have learned.

It is more places to find honey. Is it steps that lead there?

Listen to this:

The clouds move. The leaves look back to their trees wanting
more chances.

We begin cleaning

in the early hours of midnight.

The fresh air is a rush
after breathing 64

65
and a little 66 disinfectant.
We are bees. We are flowers.

Honey

The lover hummed bees before stinging swarm in his throat circling before settling down. The lover stayed away as long as he could. This is all the information available. Please go. Please go tell the lover where.

Honey

Honey save some for the jar we need to feed the others with. You go first no you go first. Your talk is setting all the bees abuzz.

Yellow

I was that flower you held
(petal among all the other petals).
Did you name me yellow flower?
Did you name me two nickels rubbed together?

Tell me
at the edge of the marsh
with the sage
and cat tails

could I grow
into a flower tree

bear
fantastic fruit

the fruit would fall
at the edge of the marsh
where animals eat and eat.

Tell me what you have named me.
Is it yellow flower, is it thin dime?

Tell me what you have learned.
Is it more places to find honey?
Is it the steps that lead there?

        In winter, the students are hunched
over their projects on the third floor mezzanine.

They eat and sleep, make love, and listen to music

plan

their projects

straight lines and curved.

                                    Some are woven.

Tiny dwellings emerge up from the tables.
Scraps drift to the floor with pencil lines, and thicker ink—
shavings scattered under some of the stools.

I use pure lemon oil
for the laminated pine tables
in the third floor library
just off the mezzanine.

          The chairs are pointed in the direction
of tiny bits of paper, detritus,
trace amounts of mud.

Mu
mud.

Ts
tsunami.

The super moon checks into this.
She is astonished. Her bombed face a perpetual O.

The afternoon proceeds in darkness.

A dry drunk Missoula afternoon
not caring whether I lived or died.
The feeling
its old stale coffee smell

in a little cupboard
where a paper bag
served as the trash.

Dickinson Street
and the unpaved part reaching up the flank
of Mt. Jumbo

where our landlord lived. Our house
still there but the fence
I used to sit on

is gone. My white halter top
borrowed from Mom
is gone, our horse, Bree,
gone

now I look

and see the trouble
I got myself into

that girl drunk
even when dry.

There is a huge panoramic map
of Malheur Field Station. It occupies
a wall on the third floor mezzanine.

The project is a study of the dwellings
and associated buildings
around the ancient lake.

The round barn,
famous for its beams
and umbrella-like structure. Other barns
and small,
government offices
depict a symmetry
not otherwise present
in the volcanic landscape.

We chose the type of winter coat
most durable. Art visits

as a strange animal
turning, checking, feeling. Art
is the butterfly

and the fur on your wings makes you a lion
beating, testing the thin air. All the flowers
in the field are men and you go to each one, tasting.
The men flowers sing their song about pollen.
Their eyes are red and their guts
are white marble from the inside of mountains
pulled out from the middle of the hills.

Now you are lifting the skirts
of women and birds and flowers
underneath the leaves of the aspens.
Green drunken curses. The sheep graze so quickly
hear

its song
singing

and looking

for Greg, now in the hospital
now out of it

his wanderings between
the buildings. How I was
supposed to walk with him
for safety

supposed to take the shortcut
and how I didn't want to go

I wanted to go my own way
down Kincaid Street

even though it wasn't as dark

it was longer
the boss said okay.
Now I walk the dark way
through the cedars
through the firs.

There's a blue light
for emergencies
and all you have to do is pull.

I thought this was the West
I have escaped to somewhere else.

And every true artist is the salvation of every other.

I thought they got on so badly as a rule.

Perhaps. But only artists produce for each other the world that is fit to live in.

—D.H. Lawrence

Mid-life dream(s) (continued)

*we have plunged down a cataract of progress which sweeps us on
into the future*
　　　—C.G. Jung

Index of dreams
as compensation for conscious
　　　　attitude
described by woman in trance,
as façade,
and immortality,
interpretation of,
—and therapy
Jung and Freud's mutual
　　　　analysis of
monotony of interpretation,
precognitive,
as psychic defenses
　and psychic transformation,

specific instances:
　　　　of phallus in subterranean
　　　　chamber,
of enlarging ball,
of enlarging telegraph wires, 18
18
of digging up bones of
prehistoric animals
of radiolarian in wood
of little light in fog
of father after his death,
of looking up at woman on
hill,
of being lost in mediaeval
building and finding idiot
child,
of girl with father complex,
of kneeling to hand girl umbrella,

of lake in woods,
of multi-storied house,
of ghost of customs official,
163
of night in Italian city,
of white dove transformed
into girl
of rows of tombs,
of great frost,

of tree transformed by frost,
of Siegfried,
of horned old man sailing
across sky ("Philemon")
    182ff

of magnolia tree on island in
Liverpool,
of alchemic books in library
of manor house near Verona
and being caught in the
        seventeenth century,
of laboratory containing fish
and reception room for spirits
of father studying fish-skin-
bound Bible, and poltergeist
phenomena

of footsteps and music at
        Bollingen Tower
of struggle with Arab prince
and book in unknown
script,
of Negro barber,
of castle of Grail,
of wife after her death,
of wife's bed as pit,

of deceased sister at garden
party,
of lecturing on life experiences
after death,

of assembly of spirits who
spoke Latin,

of dead friend learning of
psyche,

of deceased wife in Provence,

of wild Huntsman,

of father, presaging mother's
death,
of reincarnation,
of UFOs,
of yogi in chapel
dress, mother's memory of

drives, psychic,
drowning, synchronistic memory,
drum concert,
drunk, first experience of being

instances:
of escaped soul
in fount of blood in cave
of Philemon
of sailing ship on Rhine

p. 413
cases, clinical:

depressed young woman who

attempted murder of children
with infected water,

woman with paralyzed leg who
fell into spontaneous trances,

alcoholic with mother complex,

woman who confessed to murder
of friend,

old woman who made
  shoemaking movements,

Babette S., schizophrenic,

old woman who heard God's
  Voice,
girl, catatonic, who fantasied
  living on moon,

"normal" doctor who dreamed
  of being lost in mediaeval
  buildings,

man with jealous wife, who shot
  himself,
Jewish woman with apostate
  father,

theologian who dreamt of lake
  in woods,

woman who slapped her employees,
castle, golden mandala,
  of Grail, dream figure,
catatonia

Dreams (continued)

We loved the town but could not find it from underneath all the fur. Seal, reindeer, fox, wolverine, bear. The town was said to be two blocks away; past the liquor store and just by the lockers.

I knew where it was by heart. I found it in those spaces between buildings too narrow for anyone or anything else but splinters of lumber and tar paper scraps. I saw the miners going about their business, the standing around part. Summers, I found it under the boardwalk where miners lost their nuggets, their dust.

The town briefly visited during parades. These were over too soon, marching dominating Main. Kids tolerating the wait, dressed as pioneers and Okies. Kids planning their own future killings, in line for free ice cream. So patient.

About the sky
larger than the land
if that seems possible
anything could be
dry music
boats nets
baskets catching
sailors wait now
at the lone shore
their castings quiet
looking down
into the tomb
gaze across the water

Go to the currants thirsty under their newspapers
read the Umpqua Shopper while picking pods
behind the birdhouse nothing stirs grasses wait
hair-pulling strawberries already getting into it
garlic pretends not to notice what the raspberries
are doing top leaves of esteem just ask
the chocolate mint in and out of the box
over by the German chamomile it is time
to pick lettuce trim back grape vine yoga
iris tongues their sharp crisp edges
June's cedars roses lilies lavender
pale globes of fruit hard and stuck
branches stems leaves eyelashes

I was so glad to finally reach the trail
a wooden spider
witnessing the cinnamon bird
kill a friend
climbing up burnt sugar
sideways after the frothy waters

I forgot the hurricane the volcano
Nature a tired sliding becoming thinner
speckled yellow fat licking dusty skunk air

At the edge of the abyss cougar and lynx out for the view
aspen twirling weaving clouds close by the lake
It's faster at least looking up again where all the action is
it is so beautiful
spelled out
in a certain magazine

Read the owl the jackrabbit short lives narrowing
The chocolate river freely

The Butterfly's Song

1. View From Inside

This body had windows looking out over innocent lawns, old grass. An amazing pasture for large personalities. Time stood still there. The call? A large triangle, last seen dangling from the back of my chuck wagon,

ringing out across the county.

2. Butterfly Song

Flower told me what to say so I said it and nothing can be taken back now so live your marathon life and tell me what it is like at the finish, if it is cool and green as the others said along the way because they passed that on and I believed them but now just between us two—

is there something else they were describing?

3. What Was Said

To the flower or I mean about the flower, I thought was meant for me, wanted it to be. So maybe it was, after all, in that dream poetry way that is so pointed. Now it seems it maybe was my mistake, reading into things too much as I tend to do, in the wilderness

or at least close where the signage says, "you are here."

4. Wonder How

In the world this could stand just so clearly. The mountain smoldering again but in different places; wildflowers, what the butterfly

sang of long ago.

5. Booked

It never got that far—not by far! Not much said. This is my point. It was there but it did not occur. Case closed—
question mark. With the bear.

6. Mistress

The bear breathed down my neck, embracing me. I could not remember anything more intimate. Would the bear change his life for me? Highly doubtful. Would mine be different? Highly probable.

Everything is changing, everything set in motion.

7. Farms

Now in the strange valley. I know some have died for less. See this nest: only sticks and grasses, plus mud. Looking so hastily constructed. Where I land. Near the chinchilla farms.

8. Alive

I made it in and out of there alive. I turned into a noodle, a stranger. How could I say thank you and not even please in the face of this most recent transformation—

piling on so much make-up.

9. Bear Awareness

I became aware of bells tinkling, moon thought intruding, even the clouds didn't seem the same clouds as before but now the funny part:

whatever happened was going to unfold.

Conference of the Orange-crowned Warblers

This bird is one of the drabbest.
Vermivora celata of the indistinct dark eyeline
reduced or absent and therefore rarely observed
in the field. Perhaps this is why.

Vermivora celata of the indistinct dark eyeline
common to uncommon
in the field. Perhaps this is why.
Its orange crown going mostly hidden.
Common to uncommon
against the unsuspecting lawn's furious growth.
Its orange crown going mostly hidden

Common to uncommon.
What do they find to eat there?
Its orange crown going mostly hidden
in the cool damp underneath shade and shadow
in the sticky raspberry grit.

What do they find to eat there
after crossing the Cascades?
In the cool damp underneath shade and shadow
into at least Klamath
and Wasco counties.
After crossing the Cascades
into at least Klamath and Wasco counties—
what do they find to eat there
in the cool damp underneath shade and shadow?

Conference Of The Clouds

Inside might be dust or a mountain.
The clouds visible from ground level

hang

up in the air
a few hundred feet
together
their concepts
all vapor.

Thinking will change
after this softening
into a hard song.

Memoir So Far

The day was bad the horse ran away.
My memoir had to wait to live—
brambles and poison oak
were its pages.
Sticks the birch shed. What I wrote it with.
And the cover!
Clouds mixed with two parts dog
half dew
half cat
half fattened calf.

Didn't you run away once?
Fans ask this frequently.
I remember it more like chasing
in my memoir. It is my memoir after all.

It Is Bear-like

to hog
this hot
sunny day—
enjoy
summer wind
whipping the dahlias
lavender from
last summer
then mountains
hazy with smoke
not from a volcano
much difference
a world in the air
beside the Umpqua
otter tracks, river
shellfish—tiny lobsters
clams
Mom's watercolors
dreamy
of trees
mine of rocks
grasses

Too many words have burned
up like toothpicks
used on the earth's teeth
well, now
what to do? Where is
the water
convenient? The poet
scratching him her
self. Away from the table.

Studying ashes—what can transform? What becomes something else?
Under the stars, their light, I see a strange alphabet of the moon in my
hands. The word bear. A river. It is the Rogue with its twisting trail.
Day three goes through an old burn. Now, there are new trees, high

brush. The wind is wild there and far away. An osprey screams. Silence at the gravel bar, wide, open, the rocks hot.

Bears and Berries

The Umpqua, the Rogue. The country, rugged, the water soft. There are bears here and lots of willows. The river smell enthralls, drugs.

*

It is time to make red currant and raspberry jam.

*

The summer bell rings in the monastery tower all over the hillside. It is time to pray that I left enough berries for the bears.

Bear, what color are you?
A blue with white
violet rainbow
lumbers across
the green landscape
the color of a cave
the den of intention
dark matter
the most important substance
they've recently discovered
and reported in a distracted
manner way up close over there.
I've died a thousand times
at Blossom Bar
in the crashing sound
of the rapids—
their fresh mists
cooling everything
down just past
Mule Creek Canyon
and its enticing
drops into boiling pots
in the Rogue
where men have lived
hacking away at the gold

becoming ghosts
finally resting
sitting with one leg
crossed over
the other

It was suddenly crowded
in the wilderness

that summer hiking
down the Rogue River Trail.

Denise and I were visited
by our future husbands
in the guise of *Ursus americanus*—
sniffing all around the tent.
Robert Christie, Ottmar Geitner.

We managed to scare
the bear
with Sierra cups
and shouting
but it hid and waited
across Whiskey Creek
head in paws
a dog, a god
until we left
so it could really
get to know us
at least to Blossom Bar.

***

It often feels like wasted time
away from the poet's words
his dispatches
generous
greens, mauves, oranges
greys
there
the downcast eyes he goes
on and on
about...
even ellipses are fascinating
and thoroughly examined.

What is found there
is what time is all about
more or less
true. Like bears
are true.

The summer bell rings in the monastery tower all over the hillside. It is time to pray that I left enough for the bears,
The trees bend in the heat when I say this. Crushed and boiled with sugar. The country, rugged, the water soft. Although there are bears here and lots of willows. The river smell enthralls, drugs.

No Boxing Day

but the blanket toss
puts a summer feeling
on things
up in Nome—
rookeries
Sledge Island
in the far distance
gold dust on the beach
in the near
the caribou
going mad
flies
more than friendly
and the Musk Ox
sleepy
tromping near
the soft gravel bed
of eggs & milk

It Begins Then To Be Possible To Imagine

that milk falls down the mountains
perpetual flood of tears
in all the misunderstanding

between The World and Life

listen for the bridge
it is for crossing
friend peace
remember when we
worked together
because of the weather
when we used to drink there
was it frequent?
do you know if
there was honey too?

When I Became An Animal

I looked for her here but could
not quite get the smell of her,
the lay of the land even, a little
bit frozen.

River, mint, the heat
from blackberry leaves. A spirit led me
out to the rocks. It was
another sort of a game. One
a hungry critter might play.

Smelling for the past. Hearing, but
no touching. I was here. I did
not play, really. It was really
fantastic. Who could've warned me
about sadness? It was that close.

I remembered that. It did not
require much. Crawling here, a shadow there.
Spirit, flickering as we looked.

Man's West Once

> "Visions! omens! hallucinations! miracles! ecstasies, gone down the
> American river!"
> —Allen Ginsberg, "Howl"

I.
Fed by the Coloradans, I studied their ways, their trees,
and what was written on them, what was left. Names, dates.

They took me in, gave me Nescafe
instead of an Americano to-go,

> Ramona's hands arthritic
> would not straighten. Roy's
> gigantic mitts
> which knew
> irrigation and barbed wire.
> milk-marinated elk steak
> instead of Nancy's Yogurt.

That summer, I was 22 and fresh
out of college. I was given *One Man's West*,

by David Lavender. A present from Ramona.
Ramona was a summer babysitter for Little David.

Ramona's favorite book! She was mentioned,
only under another name. She was

David Lavender's biggest fan—handed everyone
copies of *One Man's West* and told about Cy Orr,

the cowboy with one eye, featured in the book,
who heard her recite "Panhandle Cob"

when she was in the second grade. After the program
Old Cy said he knew Panhandle Cob

and from then on they were friends
and she took his photo at the Boar's Nest—

with a borrowed camera,
he was on Old West treasure!

She left her May Day basket
on his porch after knocking.

His shack perched on some rocks
near the Bedrock Store, half alive
and all alone, while maggots
busily cleaned his empty socket.

.

She was so small when she was born,
they did not name her,
the youngest of eleven.
She fit in a shoe box,
set on the door of the oven,
oiled and wrapped in cotton.
Her father moved the family around
in a covered wagon.
Her father had a violin.

I loved Roy. I loved Ramona. Loved

their

photo album.
The cougars,
dead,

"Sweet Georgia Brown"
on the player piano,
played by Ramona—

Their kitchen smelled of aspic and linoleum,
failed cakes, bacon and eggs, and Delta's cottonwood air
of the old Council Tree
and of the dinosaurs' search for water—
dry, dry, as Captain John Smith's Rock House

we drove to see—Ramona's favorite place—
and her emerald eyes were startling.

From the second floor window of the old homestead
now in town, Grand Mesa's outline loomed from across
Delta's moonscape of sage and islands of alfalfa.

Roy wanted to see *The Natural*
at the Delta Drive-In. He fell asleep
just as it got interesting. But he sure knew

                                    beautiful bodies
                        all in a row at the feet of the hunters
                              who tracked them on horseback
ball games. He was a great pitcher
and two-stepper. He was the one
you wanted on the dance floor! They hated Reagan
and I was surprised. I was "the nice girl from Germany"
even though I said that was my mom, not me.
                              Roy was their guide
                              in the West Elk Mountains.

Their dog, Babe, an ancient lab
with weeping eyes. Ramona loved *The Rubiyat*

                                    with dogs—
                              visitors from Chicago
                              in the 60s and 70s
                              when there were still
                              so many.

by Omar Khayam, "the moving finger writes
and having writ, moves on..."

                              Packing them in
                              and out
                              of the wilderness.

That was Roy,
his extra income!

Being a plumber,
times were rough.
Six mouths to feed.

             I thought:
        this is the West
       I have escaped
     to somewhere else.

There was no argument
no protest, with *One Man's West*
in my possession
up at Lone Cone. I wanted

            answers
         to my questions,
       who traps whom?
     Would I be forever left
wading through the doghair aspens
    growing back so thick
      after a clear cut
     sticking to my jeans
      holding me back
     impossible to pass.

      Who is able to hear
      a cloud floating?

Hank wrote a Dear John letter
only saying:

      Whenever he appeared
      with his trusty band,
      terror reined among
      the cattle, and wrath
      and despair among
      their owners.

Dear Susan,
I am happy
with someone else.
She does her nails,
they are painted
fancy,
sharp.
We sleep together
on a mattress on the floor.
There is no home
for you
to come home to.
Stay in Colorado.

Old Lobo was a giant among wolves,
and was cunning and strong in proportion
to his size. His voice at night was well-known
and easily distinguished from his fellows.

Ramona said:
"Tell him to have at it."
when I asked for advice
about Hank.

Wild animals
become scapegoats for our own fears.
What did I have to fear?
The light stayed the same.
The city pool glistened.
Work went well
and it was
past.
It was past
time to go.

An ordinary wolf might howl
half the night about the herdsman's
bivouac without attracting more

than a passing notice, but when
the deep roar of the old king came booming
down the canyon, the watcher bestirred himself

and prepared to learn in the morning
that fresh and serious inroads
had been made among the herds.

I was afraid
of the wolf
at the door
suddenly appearing

It will be seen, then that these wolves
were thoroughly well-known to the cowboys
and shepherds.

my future
wanting in

How many of us have ever got to know
a wild animal?

begging me to feed it
more
or it would take what
it wanted
all along.

***

Our malamute was not a toy
but looked like one
when he was little
up in Nome.

I do not mean merely to meet with one once
or twice, or to have one in a cage, but to really
know it for a long time while it is wild,
and it get insight into its life and history.

I remember him running across
the tundra

hitched to a saucer
pulling Suzanne Chung
into the nowhere
of Anvil Mountain

from Chicken Hill.

>   *The trouble usually is to know one creature*
>   *from his fellow. One fox or crow is so much*
>   *like another that we cannot be sure that it really*
>   *is the same next time we meet.*

How did he get back?

>   *But once in awhile there arises an animal who is*

stronger

>   *or wiser than his fellow, who becomes a great leader,*
>   *who is, as we would say, a genius, and if he is bigger*
>   *or has some mark by which men can know him,*
>   *he soon becomes famous in his country, and*
>   *shows us that the life of a wild animal may be far*
>   *more interesting and exciting than that of many human*

How smart was she
to fall off, letting go
of the plastic handles!

>   *beings.*
>   One hundred and fifty years ago
>   the Great Plains was the richest place on Earth
>   teeming with fauna
>   quickly silenced.
>   *Of this class were Courtrand, the bob-tailed*
>   *wolf that terrorized the whole city of Paris*
>   *for about ten years in the beginning of the*
>   *fourteenth century;*

***

I was never afraid
of tornadoes. I trained myself
by lying in ditches in Missouri
just in case one would come—
and in Nome, practicing closing my mouth
and only breathing through

my nose
my babysitter said our lungs
could freeze, otherwise

> *Clubfoot; the lame grizzly bear that in two years*
> *ruined all the hog-raisers, and drove half the farmers*
> *out of business in the upper Sacramento Valley;*

snuggling inside

> *Lobo, the king-wolf of New Mexico,*
> *that killed a cow*
> *every day for five years, and the*

my wolverine ruff

> *Soehnee panther that in less than two years killed nearly*
> *three hundred human beings—and such also was* Silverspot.

on the hood
of my parka.

> *They are successful hunters not farmers.*

II.

It was a very peculiar sensation of discomfort, or frustration;
my whole body moved and stretched with unusual lightness
and strength. My arms and legs itched. My shoulders seemed
to swell; the muscles in my back and neck made me feel like pushing,
or rubbing, against trees. I felt I could demolish a wall by ramming it.

Shumagin, our husky,
could not stand it for long—the wait in the car
made him snappy.
Where is my West?
How do I find it?
Once, we got to the beach,
and let him loose,
he got into a fight
with another dog
at the party.

I was there by myself.
If something harmful
was going to happen to me,
there was no one there to help me.
I wanted to run away.

I saw how the other dog, Muchuck,
had Shumagin's eye
in his mouth
and seemed to be pulling,
pulling. I saw the optic nerve,
and some adults pouring beer
over them to stop their fighting. It dripped,
sliding to the gravel bar
in full view of the gold dredge.
Ribs from an abandoned
Quonset hut, frowning. It will be
wildly cold.
***

So many times
I imagined my other life.
A life of glass surfaces.
Easy to polish,
a cinch to wipe clean.

I had an alarming sensation
of indecision,
of not knowing what to do.

A flood of thoughts
rushed into my mind,
flashing
with extraordinary speed.

I noticed
they were rather strange thoughts;
that is, they were

strange in the sense
that they seemed to come
in a different way
than ordinary thoughts.

I read about an animal
quite unlike any other.
The information is startling
so familiar.
Who is
this strange animal?

I am familiar
with the way I think.
My thoughts
have a definite order
that is my own,

and any deviation
is noticeable.

In Nevada,
our beautiful malamute
was shot
by a neighbor.
"He was such a nuisance,"
they said, "never tied up,
always roaming."

> *One of the alien thoughts*
> *was about a statement*
> *made by an author.*
> *It was,*
> *I vaguely remember,*
> *more like a voice,*
> *or something said*
> *somewhere*
> *in the background.*

> *It happened so fast*
> *that it startled me.*

> The wolf is imaginary.
> The real one howls
> for home
> for a river
> An American river.

> *I suddenly remembered*
> *it was Alfred Kroeber.*

> Our world
> known only in photo albums?

> *Then another alien thought*
> *popped up and "said"*

that it was not Kroeber,
but Georg Simmel,
who had made the statement.

How
to win
an argument
against a gun?

I insisted it was Kroeber,
and the next
thing I knew

Are they howling
or do they
yelp?

I was in the midst
of an argument
with myself.
And had
forgotten about my feeling
of being doomed.

III.

We were taught to love everybody.

All the girls   who have flower-names   dance along
together,
and those who have not   go together also.

Our fathers
and mothers and grandfathers and grandmothers
make a place for us
where we can dance.   Each one
gathers the flower she was named for,

and then
all weave them into wreaths and crowns and scarfs
and dress up in them.

Some girls are named for rocks   and are called rock-girls,
and they find some pretty rocks which they carry; each one
such a rock as she is named for,   or whatever she is named for.
If she cannot,   she can take a branch of sage-brush,
or a bunch of rye-grass,
which have no flower.

      They all go marching along,
each girl in turn singing of herself;
but she is not a girl anymore—she is a flower singing.

Notes on "Man's West Once"

This title comes from a play on words from the book, *One Man's West*, by David Lavender, 1943, 1956, 2007. University of Nebraska, Lincoln.

Ideas in italics in Part I, are found in: Barry Lopez's, *Of Wolves And Men*, 1978. Scribner & Sons, New York. The italics also contain material found in: Ernest Seton Thomas' *Animals I Have Known*, 1898. Charles Scribner's Sons, New York.

The italics in Part II are found in Carlos Casteneda's *The Teachings of Don Juan, A Yaqui Way of Knowledge*, 1968. University of California Press, Berkeley and Los Angeles, California.

Part III is found in Sarah Winnemucca Hopkins': *Life Among The Piutes: Their Wrongs And Claims*, 1883, G.P. Putnam's Sons, New York; 1969, Chalfant Press, Inc., Sierra Media, Inc., Bishop, California.

This poem was written for Justin Hocking's Wilderness Writing course at Eastern Oregon University in 2016 when I was studying for my M.F.A. in Poetry. I got a chance to revisit strong influences in my life and memories of growing up in Nome, Alaska, Schurz, Nevada, and working in Delta, Colorado as an archeological technician one summer for the Forest Service. These are themes I write about all the time, yet Hocking elicited a unique way of untangling and addressing complex issues in the West and wanted us to take a look at the state of wolves in the West. Our readings led me back to the wild territory of my youth. I had studied with Barry Lopez, Kim Stafford, and Kate Wilhelm in the Oregon Young Writers Workshop and also with my mentor, Edward Dorn, and other fine teachers such as Lorna Dee Cervantes, Linda Hogan, Peter Michelson, Reg Saner, Marilyn Krysl, and Lucy Lippard at C.U. in Boulder in the 80s and 90s. After living in Hawaii for many years and meeting and interviewing Richard Brautigan's first wife, Virginia Brautigan Aste, I found myself circling around my old stomping grounds.

Working on new poems with Hocking, Jennifer Boyden, David Axelrod, Christopher Howell, and my thesis director, James Crews, in La Grande, Oregon (where Eastern Oregon University is located) created a protected yet wild space for my imagination and poetic wanderings, which I am forever grateful. Prose explorations with Jodi Varon and James Stolen flooded my conscious writing efforts. My co-students and visiting writers also influenced me greatly for this poem and it was with them in mind that I collaged disparate trails together for this poem. I also studied Melissa Kwasny, Danielle Deulen, Piotr Florczyk, Larisa Sporzluk, Tom Clark, Edward Dorn, Duncan Jones, and Jonathan Chant's poetry and scholarship during this time in order to catch a listen of their howls.

Interesting conversations with Megan Kruse also led me to this work when I told her about volunteering in Maupin, Oregon, for the Bureau of Land Management.

Acknowledgements:

"Mezzanine" was informed by conversations with architecture student, Andrew Loia, at the University of Oregon, Lawrence Hall. Thanks for talking about the mezzanine with me. Also much thanks to the Lawrence Hall students who work so industriously during the night and who provided inspiration for me and my creative work. Thanks, William Lien!

"Mezzanine" was also inspired by an exhibit of Josef Albers' book plates from *Interaction of Color* that I viewed in the Hayden Gallery, Lawrence Hall, in 2016. Grateful acknowledgement is given to the University of Oregon, and to the College of Design, and especially to professors Esther Hagenlocher and Landry Smith, who curated and designed the exhibit, respectively, and who generously submitted to my questions.

Albers, Josef. *Interaction of Color.* Yale University Press, 1963.

"Color, A Magic Power." Exhibition of Josef Albers' selected plates, acrylic on paper. University of Oregon, 2016.

Salter, Michael, "Elements of Time" mural display in foyer of Lawrence Hall, University of Oregon by Salter and his students. Viewed 2015-2018.

"Mid-life dream(s) (continued)" found in: *Memories, Dreams, Reflections,* Index, pp. 416-418, C.G. Jung, 1963. Pantheon Books.

Poems appearing here have been published in the following in slightly different form: *Barrow Street Press 4 X 2 Project, Caliban Online, Carolina Quarterly, Mojave River Review, Rain Bird, Timothy McSweeney's Internet Tendency,* and *Tom Clark Beyond the Pale.*

Thanks to the Eastern Oregon University Foundation and the La Grande community for their support. Thanks to my teachers and student cohort at Eastern Oregon University for help with poems in this manuscript. I would especially like to thank James Crews, Jennifer Boyden, David Axelrod, Jodi Varon, Christopher Howell, James

Stolen, Justin Hocking, and Megan Kruse. Thanks to Susan Moore, Melissa Kwasny, M.L. Smoker, Lidia Yuknavitch, Piotr Florczyk, and other visiting writers. Thanks to my cohort: Theresa Hamman, Zinn Adeline, Skyler Avery, Amelia Zahm, Asha Dore, Tavia Mendez, Liz Asch, Beverly Reid, Jim Benton, Debbie Bone, Larry King, (Kate King), Aaron Byers, Steven Jackson, Samuel Temple, Katelyn Presley, Alexis Smith, Carol Horwath Fischbach, Amy Parker, and Althea Huesties-Wolf & family.

Thanks to the Prineville District Bureau of Land Management for allowing me to volunteer at the Depot House in Maupin, Oregon, in the summer of 2015. Thanks to Lost Horse Press for the internship in the winter of 2016. Thanks to Debbie Carson for her hospitality in La Grande.

Thanks to Virginia Brautigan Aste, Mara Aste, and family, Sandra Krawciw and family, Brenda Kasani, Shawna K. Rudio, Ethan Windahl, Wilma Geitner, Frank Bruestle, Gerhard Oshmann, and their families. Thanks Jim Cartwright, Carol Morris, Diane Wakoski, and Annie Davidovich. Thanks, Ingrid Wendt. Much thanks to the Colrain Intensive and to Fred Marchant, Martha Rhodes, Rusty Morrison, and Joan Houlihan. Thanks to Marcy Albin Horne and family.

Thanks to my parents and sisters & their families for their support over the years and to my husband, Ottmar Geitner, and our daughters, Carola and Mareike. Thanks to my aunties and uncles in America and in Germany and also to my cousins. Thanks to my niece and nephews. Thanks to Elvina Douglas Naranjo for helping raise me. Thanks, Brenda Kasani, for that too.

Thanks to the Ragdale Foundation for a writing residency, the Student Conservation Association for internships to Alaska and Colorado, The Anderson Ranch Center For the Arts for Margaret Durrance photojournalism scholarships, National Poetry Series, and thanks to Hank Trotter, Jerry Greene, and Adam Liu and their families for their support. Thanks to Alan McNarie, Lillian Cunningham, Tom Peek, Marcia Hee, and Patti Epler. Thanks Julie Mitchell and her book club.

Thanks Jasmine Ginter. Thanks Jinah Janus. Thanks Rae Yamanaka. Thanks Angelica Heinegg Clark. Thanks Doreen Kamakea. Thanks so much too, to Jonathan Chant, Duncan Jones, and Nin Andrews for cheering me on during my blog's early years.

Thanks Jennifer Dunbar Dorn, Maya Dorn and family, Linda Hogan, Lorna Dee Cervantes, Peter Michelson, Reg Saner, David Simpson, Reed Bye, Marilyn Krysl, and Lucy Lippard. Thanks Sandra McRae Sajbel and Carolyn Hart. Thanks to the University of Colorado-Boulder for a Fellowship. Thanks Leah Bradley and C.J. Roffis. Thanks Ingrid Wendt. Thanks to Coleman Stevenson, Owner, The Dark Exact. Thanks, Inga Schruttke.

Thanks to my supervisors: Michael A. Harwood, Jeff Butler, Kevin Farthing, Michael Philley, Tim Winder, Stan Singer, and Nicholas R. Grant; and to the Lillis Key Box Graveyard Shift Crew for their support during the writing of this book.

Ed Dorn, Tom Clark, Denise Hall, Robert Christie, Ramona & Roy Hawk, Sandra Krawciw, Katherine Thalberg, Pacomio Chacon, and Greg Brenner—*in memorium.*

Susan Kay Anderson, National Poetry Series Finalist, has recent work in *Barrow Street Press 4 X 2 Project, Beat Scene, Caliban Online, Concise, Tom Clark Beyond The Pale*, and other publications. Her honors include fellowships from the University of Colorado, Ragdale, Anderson Ranch Center for the Arts, Student Conservation Association, an American Intercultural Field Service Exchange to Finland, and year abroad at the University of Tuebingen. She grew up in Nome, Missoula, Reno, and Germany, among other places, before studying at the University of Oregon and then at the University of Colorado, where her master's thesis was directed by Edward Dorn. She worked as a bookseller at Explore Books in Aspen, a barista in Honolulu, and an archeological technician in Oregon, Colorado, Alaska, and Hawaii before serving as a secondary and post-secondary educator in Hawaii for twenty years. She lives in Eugene, Oregon, and recently completed an M.F.A. in Creative Writing at Eastern Oregon University. Her poetry blog is: *Hawaii Teacher Detective.*